T0368075

The Road of Righteousness

Christian Poetry Devotional

SHELLEY SAFRIT

WESTBOW
PRESS®
A DIVISION OF THOMAS NELSON
& ZONDERVAN

WestBow Press books may be ordered through booksellers or by contacting:

WestBow Press
A Division of Thomas Nelson & Zondervan
1663 Liberty Drive
Bloomington, IN 47403
www.westbowpress.com
844-714-3454

ISBN: 979-8-3850-4087-2 (sc)
ISBN: 979-8-3850-4086-5 (e)

Library of Congress Control Number: 2024927125

Print information available on the last page.

WestBow Press rev. date: 02/06/2025

Dedicated to Jesus,
my Savior!

I said to the LORD,
"You are my Lord;
apart from You I have
no good thing."

Psalm 16:2 BSB

May these words, given during
my quiet times with our LORD,
be an encouragement and a source of hope.

May you find your strength
in the One
Who knows you best,

Jesus...

Contents

The Road of Righteousness

There is no other road, there is no other way,
There is no other righteousness, none other can display.
Jesus is the only way to find Truth and Light,
He is the only One Who died to save your life.

Come to Him, let Him in,
He alone forgives sin.
Change your ways to His alone,
His Word will teach your very soul.

His Holy Spirit will lead and guide,
His faithfulness will flow from His side.
Then He will cover you with His righteousness,
The road will be clear, full of His faithfulness.

No other Name, no other way,
Won't you let Him clothe you day after day?
Open your heart to His love and grace,
Let Him cover you with His loving embrace.

Let Him change your ways,
You will never be the same.
A grateful heart full of praise,
As you find He is the only way!

If you desire to receive Jesus as your Savior, write your name and the date below.
Pray, "Thank You Heavenly Father for sending Your Son, Jesus to die on the cross for my sins. Jesus, I ask You to forgive me of my sins and to please help me to live for You. Teach me to grow in You and Your righteousness through Your Holy Spirit, as I read Your Word, and seek Your truth, love, and the plans You have for my life. In Jesus' Name I ask and pray. Amen."

_____

Your Name   Date

"For God so loved the world, that he gave his only Son, that whoever believes in him should not perish but have eternal life."
John 3:16 ESV

1

No Man

No man on earth,
No matter the search,
Can forgive sin,
And live within,
The mystery of the heart.

Where Jesus is known,
And His righteousness is sown,
Where a heart grows,
And continually knows,
God has set him apart.

To honor and behold,
A glory only known,
To the one who cleaves,
To Jesus Who never leaves,
Our Priest and High King forever.

Who forgives our sin,
So we can walk with Him,
And live our days,
Following His ways,
No other will there be, no not ever.

"We have this as a sure and
steadfast anchor of the soul,
a hope that enters into the
inner place behind the curtain,
where Jesus has gone as a
forerunner on our behalf, having
become a high priest forever
after the order of Melchizedek."
Hebrews 6:20 ESV

Jesus Lover of My Soul

Jesus lover of my soul,
How I long to be with you,
You will lead me safely home,
You will lead me to Your throne.

In my heart where You dwell,
You tell me all is well.
I release to You my soul,
You come in and make me whole.

Though this world is dimly lit,
And my life is so short lived.
I will walk upon the earth,
Sharing You and Your rebirth.

And when You do call me home,
I will stand before Your throne.
I will look into Your face,
Every sorrow You'll erase.

When I see Your kingdom come,
And Your will on earth is done.
Every treasure will be made known,
All glory given to You alone.

For when we see the King of kings,
And lay our crowns at Your feet,
Washed by Your blood, O Holy Lamb,
We'll live and move in the Great I AM!

"Hallelujah!
Sing a new song to the Lord.
Sing his praise in the assembly of godly people."
Psalm 149:1 GW

From Old to New

As I glanced across the ground,
Death and destruction stood deliberate and profound.
Dry and lifeless, unkempt and stayed,
I wondered where the truth did lay.

Then a green shoot caught my eye,
And I watched it as the weeks went by.
For this precious seed spread up toward the light,
Growing strong both day and night.

Then finally it revealed its appearance,
Petals of beauty drew delicate nearness.
Displaying such detail by sketch and design,
Its Maker was truly one of a kind.

For He with His loving majestic care,
Brought forth beauty from a ground of despair!
A perfect creation, flawless and full,
A perfect plan with purpose and goodwill.

If He can do this from the dirt He laid forth.
Imagine the limitless lives He can restore.
When we allow the seed of His Word inside,
He will cleanse us from sin and darkness that hides.

No longer locked down by the chains of this earth,
But released, a new creation, born again by His rebirth.

"Therefore, if anyone is in Christ, he is a new creation. The
old has passed away; behold, the new has come."
2 Corinthians 5:17 ESV

Shaken, Yet Held in Your Hand

When things are shaken and fall apart,
Jesus remains in my heart.
Where human glories fail and cease,
These will not bother me.

The things of this world will roll away,
And its cares will never stay.
For in time, one day they will be shaken,
All unrighteousness sifted, forsaken,
Away, to be gone forever,
And the tares separated, severed.

For all who stand this heavenly shake,
Will remain in Him, and partake,
Of the beauties and mysteries yet to be,
Seen throughout life with Jesus in eternity.

Where no man can ever touch or shake,
The child of God who chooses to take,
The hand of our God Who is awesome and strong,
Whose foundation will never be gone.

Who choose to give their lives to Him,
He protects through His blood, even when shaken.

"Therefore let us be grateful for receiving a
kingdom that cannot be shaken..."
Hebrews 12:28 ESV

Waiting

Wind powerfully pounding day after day,
Trees mournfully moaning in swathe and sway.
Electric lightning striking trees in two,
Blackness burns unscathed portions through.

Flourishing *forests* flowing, yet choking with thorns,
Their sharpness grappling, causing woe and mourn.
Clenching but winding, quietly down and around,
Thick thirsty thorns remove beauty without a sound.

Tumultuous, tempest raging *seas*,
Storm splitting, throwing waves to their knees.
Pounding, protruding onto the riddled shore,
A continual release, with rest no more.

Precious *prairies* holding tearful terrible thistles.
So densely, so thickly, the wind causes a whistle.
Splendor desires to separate, but the beauty will be marred,
Unraveling the scene, leaving it scarred.

All of *creation* longs for release,
From the tares of sin, devastation and disease.
God sees and knows, and He will return,
To fully restore wheat that yearns.

"His winnowing fork is in his hand, and he will clear
his threshing floor and gather his wheat into the barn,
but the chaff he will burn with unquenchable fire."
Matthew 3:12 ESV

God Continues Our Journey

I'm at a halt.
But You are not.
You're always moving to make a way,
So, I'll continue to walk with You all day.

Words, no words,
But Your Word is strong,
Living and powerful to carry on.
Thorough in correction, dividing right from wrong.

Stuck, but secure,
Unsure of surroundings.
But You know the heart's deepest reserves.
You guide the path, You know the twists and turns.

Free, anywhere in grace,
Where sin is forgiven and erased.
Your will be done, I follow You,
Questions answered when I see anew.

"For this light momentary affliction is preparing for us an eternal
weight of glory beyond all comparison, as we look not to the things
that are seen but to the things that are unseen. For the things that
are seen are transient, but the things that are unseen are eternal."
2 Corinthians 4:17,18 ESV

Given to God

Quietly sits in God's plan,
Is unlike any other man.
Rests in the stillness of the wait,
Pondering things that come his way.

Meditates, contemplates to this end,
Daily tasks seem to transcend.
Into God's unique and perfect plan,
He walks with Him over and again.

Therefore, time does not slip away,
For God renews his purpose day by day.
And in this perfect plan he stays,
Following the Savior, he steadily remains.

For the path meanders unchanged,
And the end will remain the same.
When the final day has come,
His hope will reveal God's own son.

"...But I am not ashamed, for I know whom I have
believed, and I am convinced that he is able to guard
until that day what has been entrusted to me."
2 Timothy 1:12 ESV

God's Purpose Restored!

Like a tethered leash established in the ground,
The lion walked round and round.
Tirelessly pacing back and forth,
Longing desperately for something more.
Steel fences held him back,
But inside these, he suffered no lack.
No need of attack, nor to count the cost,
His prey not needed; his vision lost.

But one day the gate opened and remained,
His heart throbbed; he readied his legs.
Forging ahead, power on land,
He gathered strength, he ran and ran.
Into the treacherous desert terrain,
So glad to be home once again.
His senses racing, his intelligence heightened,
Ready to pounce, not even once frightened.
Instinct enabled by ranges to roam,
Ready for purpose, a place called home.

Now free to live again,
And be the fear of all men.
Shared respect, born for more,
King of the beasts created to roar!

"I know that you can do all things, and that
no purpose of yours can be thwarted."
Job 42:2 ESV

No Longer a Slave

Fearful of making meaningless mistakes,
And being pleasing for only man's sake.
I know deep down inside,
In human plans I cannot reside.

But this way is wearing me down,
Myself, I've lost, longing to be found.
Tired of needless expectations,
Tripping over many frustrations.

So, to You, my soul I do lift,
I know only You can release these iron grips.
Break every link in this chain,
So only You and I remain.

Remake me as Your hand makes the clay,
So, I can live in Your freedom, day after day.
With borders impassable and strong,
Unafraid to step forth, to travel on.

And I will love you completely through,
So, all will see me enraptured in You!
Your boundaries surround me, in You I stand,
Your love and power surpass mere man!

Leaving bondage to cling no more,
Gratefully delighted for all You restore.
Into the purpose and beautiful plan,
Where I safely reside in the palm of Your hand.

"Behold, I have engraved you on the palms of my
hands: your walls are continually before me."
Isaiah 49:16 ESV

I Know You are Good

When the sun fades into the night,
And the days are no longer bright.
It is then You draw so near,
Even though the way unclear.

Because Your promises hold so true,
Each morning Your mercies are new.
And when I can't see the way,
You give light for my path each day.

You never leave nor forsake,
My enemies flaunt but with You I partake.
I taste and I see,
That You are all I truly need.

Why?...Because God, **I know You are good,**
Everything in this world, You withstood.
You took the punishment of sin for me,
All that is good rests in Thee...

"The Lord is good to all and His mercies are over all His works."
Psalm 145:9 NASB

In His Shadow

Silently leading others to stay,
Along the straight and narrow way.
To rest quietly at the Savior's side,
Within His words to gracefully abide.

To always gently remember,
To sit and talk to Jesus, so tender.
Here, He delicately comes so close,
He reveals Himself through the shadows.

Making us holy as He is,
Separating us for such a time as this.
For the days are short and oh, so fast,
But at His feet, His winnowing will last.

So kindly, so sweetly, rest softly with Him.
The beauty of His gaze will never end.
For the wonder of this narrow way,
Is following Jesus day after day...

He who dwells in the shelter of the Most High, will
abide in the shadow of the Almighty.
Psalm 91:1 ESV

Unveiled

Once I was in the dark,
The veil pulled over my heart.
Walking around with no sight,
Without understanding, alone in the night.

Then one day, I came to Him,
To ask Him to come in,
Into my heart where the veil, He removed,
Now He resides in my inner room.

Here, He lovingly lights my way,
Continually day after day.
My sight, clean and clear,
As I draw softly near.

To the One Who died for me,
So, I could be released and free.
Drawn near, by His Spirit,
Resting being oh so near Him!

Never alone, always I'll be,
Worshipping the One Who tore the veil so I could see.
The only true God in the depths of my heart,
All because of the veil He tore apart!

But when one turns to the Lord, the veil is removed. Now the Lord
is the Spirit, and where the Spirit of the Lord is, there is freedom.
2 Corinthians 3:16-17 ESV

The Cup

And going a little farther he fell on his face and prayed, saying,
"My Father, if it be possible, let this cup pass from me;
nevertheless, not as I will, but as you will."
Matthew 26:39 ESV

The cup set before Him, His own desire laid aside,
With an **iron** will to obey and abide.

Eyes opened from prayer, looking around,
Everyone was **asleep** on the ground.
Not one could stay awake,
For soon the Son of God they'd take.

Then came a taunting distasteful kiss,
From a close companion of His.
The **gesture** left disdainful taste,
His reward stood as such a waste.

Betrayal came from a passionate friend,
Causing the rooster to crow thrice over again.
For the accuser thought he was one of His,
But their accusations, he dismissed!

A crown of thorns crushed into his head,
All whom he loved, completely **fled**.
The burden of sin upon His shoulders
Nails pounded by Roman soldiers.

He hung on the cross against the sky,
Here He made His final cry.
He said, "Father **forgive** them for they know not what they do."
Here He became the way for all men to know the Truth.

As the Son of God hung his head,
They realized He was dead.
The spear pierced His side,
Blood and water, the **crimson** tide.

But on the third day He arose,
He **conquered** death and every foe.
Word spread, and as He said,
He arose from the dead!

For now, the love of God is known,
So, through Jesus, God could make us his own.
The only Truth that will lead you home.
Salvation found in Him alone.

The cup set before Him, His own desire laid aside,
Will you **now** lay down your own will and come and abide?
In Jesus.

"As the time drew near for his return to heaven, he moved
steadily onward toward Jerusalem with an iron will.
Luke 9:51TLB

But to all who did receive him, who believed in his name,
he gave the right to become children of God.
John 1:12 ESV

His Purpose

Are you able to go through life,
And not question any strife?
Knowing that this world will fade,
Into the new one God has made?

And when logic seems out of sorts,
To God's Word can you resort?
For things of this world are understood,
When clearly looked upon in God's Word.

So, when the road winds and turns,
Look for wisdom to be learned.
By leaning not on your own reason,
But taking His hand in every season.

And when the unknown is unclear,
Look to Jesus and draw near.
For the riches of His grace continually flow,
And His purpose He will make known.

He stores up sound wisdom for the upright; he is
a shield to those who walk in integrity.
Proverbs 2:7 ESV

Beauty of Righteousness

Rightly divide the Word of Truth,
And Jesus will abide in you.
Growing fruits of righteousness,
Ready to spread His loving kindness.

Releasing forgiveness into His hands,
Walking humbly in a fallen land.
Loving mercy to no end,
Carrying gentleness as a close friend.

Looking for justice for a coming kingdom,
Kneeling in prayer for others to seek Him.
Knowing His blood covers our sin,
Knowing He is the only way in...

To a place full of beauty fully unscathed,
Let His righteousness cloth all your ways.
Cleaving unto His joy of being born again,
For this is His gift given to all men.

If you know that he is righteous, you may be
sure that everyone who practices righteousness
has been born of him.
1 John 2:29 ESV

Ageless

When age has come,
And the beauties thereof,
Your loveliness never fades.
When eyes are dim,
And steps lessen,
You lengthen our days.

When hearing eases,
And quietness appeases,
Your voice I will hear.
For strength for the weak,
And hope for the least,
Is why You draw near.

Although the aged seems poor,
There is surety and so much more,
We cling to what we know.
So soon we will be,
Forever in eternity,
Where heaven's beauties flow.

Dressed in white,
With complete sight,
Radiance all around.
With strength anew,
And hearing too!
What was lost now is found!

For God's time has no border,
His ways, fully ordered,
A thousand years roll into one.
In patience and love,
He nurtures from above,
And one day is a thousand years done.

But do not overlook this one fact, beloved, that with the Lord one
day is as a thousand years, and a thousand years as one day.
2 Peter 3:8 ESV

Return

He went astray,
He wandered away.
Caught in the world's cares,
Living among the tares.

Run to the one who is this way,
Rescue him, who is lost today.
For God does not want him ambling along,
Continually choosing what is wrong.

Don't give up, but fervently pray,
Encouraging him day after day.
Helping him, come what may,
He will see you're anchored and completely stayed.

Pray in hope he will come back,
Although long suffered from many attacks.
His eyes opened seeing the truth,
May he come to Jesus, pray him through.

For one day he will thank you,
And to you no payment will be due.
Only to love the next person through,
Only to know, that could have been you.

My brothers, if anyone among you wanders from
the truth and someone brings him back,
let him know that whoever brings back
a sinner from his wandering will save his soul
from death and will cover a multitude of sins.
James 5:19-20 ESV

Words that Build

Days of complaints will fly like wings,
As well as words full of sting.
Time is short and days are few,
Words should glisten like the morning dew.

For in the end things will remain,
That are golden, purified, and unstained.
Treasure stored up above,
Spoken willingly because of love,

Are you like wood, stubble, hay or grass?
Only refining words will last.
Words that bless will be words that stay,
All else burned, tested through fire, gone away.

But words of beauty will fly away,
Into God's hands where they will remain.
These golden treasures are Heaven's scent
Hope released and encouragement.
A flitting word, a timely manner,
Resounds aloud, in glorious grandeur.

While time draweth nigh,
Let pleasantries flow from deep inside,
To glorify our God on earth,
Never knowing where His seed doth work.

Now if anyone builds on the foundation with gold, silver, precious
stones, wood, hay, straw— each one's work will become manifest,
for the Day will disclose it, because it will be revealed by fire,
and the fire will test what sort of work each one has done.
1 Corinthians 3: 12-13 ESV

Reason

Come, where has your reason gone,
Humble yourself to see the wrong.
God is the Maker of all things,
And assuredly lives in hearts who worship Him.

Look into the brilliant night sky,
Scattered but ordered, do you know why?
Inside of you, you know there is something more,
Let go of and lie down the continual tug of war.

Relinquish your soul to the One who knows,
Each star that shines and every grain of sand the wind blows.
For the crimson tide,
Which flowed from his side.
Brought forgiveness of sin,
And placed purity deep within.

For the One Who tells the storm to stop,
Securely holds every tear we drop.
And places Himself in the heart of man,
Oh, His name is the great I AM!

Come now, let us reason together, says the
Lord: though your sins are like scarlet,
they shall be as white as snow; though they are red
like crimson, they shall become like wool.
Isaiah 1:18 ESV

Wake Up, My Heart

Where has your heart gone?
By this world, it has lingered on.
Forgetting the Only source of life,
It moved away in dark nights.

But Jesus' love is oh, so kind,
He comes close to look inside.
And seeing you have moved a little far away,
He draws you back, will you stay?

For the Holy Spirit calls, He softly beckons,
For you to come to His feet and tenderly listen.
For in the stillness of the night,
He breaks through, gentle and quiet.

To light the path and always be,
Faithfully, lovingly calling to thee.
And here you never have to move away,
His purpose will be fulfilled in you each day.

So, today afresh and anew,
Rise, for He affectionately waits for you.
His mouthpiece, His vessel, His potted clay,
Fit for our Father's use, day after day…

Teach me to do your will, for you are my God! Let
your good Spirit lead me on level ground!
Psalm 143: 10 ESV

Goodness of God

Do you see someone oh, so kind,
Who only has Jesus on his mind,
Who loves to do good each day,
And seems determined in all his ways?

Loving others wherever they may be,
Reaching out showing love and mercy.
Serving with tender care,
Letting others know Jesus is there.

Giving of themselves without care or thought,
Only doing what Jesus has taught.
Spreading His message for all to know,
Jesus is the only way to go.

And the goodness of God overflows,
From him who does His work wherever he goes.

Do not neglect to do good and to share what you have,
for such sacrifices are pleasing to God.
Hebrews 13:16 ESV

Love Your Brother

How hard it is to love your brother,
When you see him with sins uncovered?
When you live within his range,
And see hypocrisy and speech untamed.

Without care of measuring His Word,
To what is said, is absurd.
Hurt reflected from unfurled faces,
Caught between trespassed spaces.

For God's Word should abide,
And be leaned on heavily from every side.
Prayer should light the way each day,
Relying on God as we rightly walk His way.

Where criticism is left behind,
Replaced with wisdom that refines.
And love, oh love that drops away,
Every sin that stumbles our way.

Covering anticipations that can instantly change,
Causing true newness day after day.
Where world and hate can be wiped away,
And all will see peculiarity displayed.

Living as His pilgrims on this earth,
For we are His body, His holy church.

And this commandment we have from him: whoever
loves God must also love his brother.
1 John 4:21ESV

Radiance of Grace

Through the sunshine through the rain,
And through every single windowpane,
God's love shines completely through.
Waiting quietly for me and you.

Coming in oh, so close,
Whether the panes are opened or closed.
His love penetrates, presses in,
Washing, cleansing, forgiving sin.

Revealing acceptance, purpose, and grace,
His love overflows, a precious place.
Here in our hearts His love consumes us,
And we find ourselves filled with His purpose.

So we have come to know and to believe the
love that God has for us. God is love, and whoever
abides in love abides in God, and God abides in him.
1 John 4:16 ESV

Where Would I Be?

O the beauty and mystery,
Of knowing the One Who created me.
Who knew me before time began,
O the joy of Your perfect plan!

For when I wasn't seen or even heard.
You provided a way for another birth.
Through Your Holy Spirit's faithfulness,
Who lives in me because You took my place,
On the cross for my sinfulness,
You died so I could live in Your holiness.

You invited me to become a pilgrim in this world,
To be protected through Your Holy Word.
To learn how loving and kind you are!
You provide wisdom I need, as my Heavenly Father.

O where would I be without You by my side?
Where would I be if I couldn't abide?
Lost in a whirlwind in an earthly place,
With no hope of a future in Your Heavenly gates.

Every breath You give to me,
And You are every breath I breathe.
My heart is Yours I love none other,
O thank you my Father for sending Your Son...Jesus.

The Spirit of God has made me,
and the breath of the Almighty gives me life.
Job 33:4 ESV

Restorer

In quietness, in my soul,
You cover me and make me whole.
It is where I find You true,
Where You make all things new.

So, in Your loving arms I hide,
Completely safe, I abide.
I rest before Your holy throne,
I ponder my one true home.

For in the still small voice, I find.
Your Words so gentle, and oh so kind.
I give my times to You alone,
Your will in me, You make known.

To walk with You each day,
Looking for you in quietness stayed.
You alone, lover of my soul,
Your peace restores me, You overflow.

So, each morning as I rise,
And watch Your faithfulness greet the skies.
I know You're providing yet another day,
And You alone are the only way.

The LORD said, "Go out and stand on the mountain in the presence of the LORD, for the LORD is about to pass by." Then a great and powerful wind tore the mountains apart and shattered the rocks before the LORD, but the LORD was not in the wind. After the wind there was an earthquake, but the LORD was not in the earthquake. After the earthquake came a fire, but the LORD was not in the fire. And after the fire came a gentle whisper.
1 Kings 19:11,12 NIV

Expectations

When expectations are too high,
And you cannot find the wings to fly,
Know you are not held in chains,
But held by the One Who forever reigns.

In this life this world can become,
A ball and chain and burdensome,
But the only One you need to please,
Is the One Who brings you close, while on your knees.

For in this time with Jesus lies,
Peace without compromise,
A knowing that you are completely loved,
You are wholly accepted by God's own Son,
And no one can ever take that away,
You are not alone, not even for one day.

God's plan and purpose for you,
Is to trust He always has His best for you.
For the cares of this world will soon be gone,
But your life with Jesus will continue on.

So never doubt His love for you,
Cling to His Word, the only Truth,
Look to Him alone to please,
And keep loving Him on your knees.

Let no one despise you for your youth, but set the
believers an example in speech, in conduct, in love, in
faith, in purity... Do not neglect the gift you have...
1 Timothy 4:12,14 ESV

Captain of Our Waters

When the sun lies over the edge of the waters,
It's held in the hand of our Father.
Settling in for the night to rest,
Where you can lovingly trust.

Jesus to keep your waters calm,
He will still them without alarm.
Always teaching you the way to go,
He leads in truth, all things He knows.

When waters are rough,
And days are tough,
Only seek His guide.

He will never fail,
Not in any gale,
Because for you He died.

The narrow way is hidden in Him and never hard to find,
Only come and listen where He says, "You are mine."
For His Name covers yours,
Because you stand along His shore.

So through your days and His beautiful ocean waves,
He will always be your Captain, who saved...
You!

Enter through the narrow gate. For wide is the gate and broad
is the road that leads to destruction, and many enter through
it. But small is the gate and narrow is the road that leads to
destruction, and many enter through it. But small is the gate
and narrow the road that leads to life, and only a few find it.
Matthew 7:13,14 NIV

Everyone was amazed. "What kind of man is this?" they
said. "Even the winds and the waves obey him!"
Matthew 8:27 GNT

Do You Know Your One True Friend?

More important than a son or daughter,
For like a lamb He was slaughtered.
More important than anything,
That is why Jesus should be your friend.

For to truly know Him,
Is to genuinely accept Him.
It is to sincerely understand His deep love,
And take seriously our heavenly Father's only Son,

So, live for Him,
In the midst of sin.
Because in the end,
He will win.

To be on His side,
Where righteousness abides.
Is the only safe place,
For none will escape...

...the coming judgement, yes and amen,
Unless you let Jesus save you, my friend.
Draw near, come to Him,
Only He will take you where eternity never ends.

Call on His name from a pure heart,
He will save you when this world falls apart.
Your relationship with Him, a desperate and dire need.
If your heart is full of Him, He is your Friend indeed!

You are my friends if you do what I command you.
John 15:14 ESV

Will You Say Yes?

Your years,
Will bring Him near,
To have and to hold,
Until you grow old.
Will you say yes?
This is no test.
Your life is at stake,
You are not fully awake.

Blind to the unseen,
Living unknowingly for any means.
Unreasoning that you are dead,
Until you understand what Jesus said.
Repent from your worldly ways,
For the commandments show where sin lays.
For you cannot keep even one,
Unless you take the hand of God's only Son.

He will lead you, He is the door.
Where you will be ashamed no more.
Fully forgiven and entered in,
Here, you become born again.
Seeing the world as it is,
Strayed and stayed and stuck in bliss.
But now you see, you have overcome.
You have said yes to God's only Son.

You are His bride His one true love,
Soon the marriage that matters is going to come.
Will you be with Him dressed in white,
Forever loving Him, at His side?

Eternally forever, to have and to hold,
Where you will never ever grow old.
Be ready!

Behold, he is coming with the clouds, and every eye will
see him, even those who pierced him, and all tribes of the
earth will wail on account of him. Even so. Amen.
Revelation 1:7 ESV

Few

Minutes are few,
Much left to do.
World sleeping,
Causes weeping.
By those who know,
The way to go.
Who speak in truth,
But are refused.
They watch with tears,
Through the years.
And yet will anyone come?

With hand to the plow,
And rescue needed now.
They continue in toil,
To nourish the soil.
Preaching the Gospel,
To the bleak and hostile.
For that is God's will,
So, they continue still.
Never in vain,
Is the blood stain.
Yes, they will come!

Whether with words,
Or actions heard.
Come many or few,
They will be new.
Minutes pass,
His Word will last.
So be ready,
Faithfully steady.
Lift Him tall,
He was crushed for us all.
God's Son has won!

And he said to them, "Go into all the world and proclaim the gospel
to the whole creation. Whoever believes and is baptized will be
saved, but whoever does not believe will be condemned."
Mark 16:15-16 ESV

You are Watching Over Me

Alone, I am not,
Never in want.
Even in the night season,
I yield to Your reason.
You are at my side,
I release, I abide.
You are my light,
I give You my fight.
I will overcome,
My heart is winsome.
Completely Yours,
You restore and even more.
My soul alight,
In You alone, I delight.
Your cross lifted high,
I ponder, all is nigh.
It is finished,
Your love never diminished.
I will rest in Your care,
You will never go anywhere.
So, I will wait,
I will not hesitate.
I give You my life,
Hidden in Christ.
Safe in everything,
Now, forever, and whatever You bring.

You, LORD, keep my lamp burning;
my God turns my darkness into light.
Psalm 18:28 NIV

A Mother's Days

She sits at the table, saying prayers,
For her children, who know she cares.
Reading each name into God's Word,
With confidence, her voice will be heard.

Then she kneels and raises her hands,
To leave them in God's holy plan.
Quietly, she ponders her love for them,
Prayers flow over and again.

As she prostrates herself before the throne,
She pleads with Jesus, they will make it home.
Where the joy of life will never end,
Where they will see that Jesus was their closest Friend.

She stands up and looks afar,
For that is where her treasures are.
Within her, God's holiness dwells,
So, she will continue to pray, to tell.

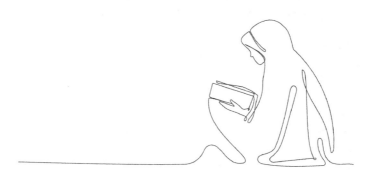

For the LORD is good and
his love endures forever;
his faithfulness continues through all generations.
Psalm 100:5 NIV

By His Side

Snuggled in and set apart,
That is where God has your heart.
Here you can safely cling,
To the one who created your being.

He reaches down with His arms,
To give you peace, through alarm.
To comfort your heart through the days,
And remain with you constant, and always.

No matter what comes your way,
God and His love will continually stay.
By your side attending you,
Forever faithful, steadfastly true.

...for he has said, "I will never leave you nor forsake you."
Hebrews 13:5 ESV

Begin

With this world's sorrows and this world's sways,
Where does your foundation lay?
Is it built upon the Rock?
And does it stand within His flock?

Where you can enter and be saved,
By the One Who rose from the grave.
And learn to live and move in Him,
To take His hand and call Him, Friend.

To deepen your roots in His Word, His power,
As He gives you strength hour by hour.
Surrendering to Him, your One true love,
Out of pure desire to live through Jesus, God's own Son.

Loving His journey, knowing the end,
Is the very reason to begin...

Your Word is a lamp unto my feet,
and a light unto my path.
Psalm 119:105 ESV

Blessings Unseen

Leaves are the footprints you can see,
But blessed is the one who never saw
what the disciples did see.

For even though you have never seen and
even though you have never heard,
My Spirit is in you, your vision unblurred.

You've already set, your mind on things above,
Walk forward with Me and I will show you My love,

To bring to a world filled with the poor,
To unveil My riches of so much more.

For the beauty of this earth can never compare,
To the things unseen of which you are aware.

And though the day brings the night,
Everything you see is a glimpse of My might.

Revealed to the chosen, devoted, and true,
Who walk along the narrow path in My view.

Following the only way there is to live,
Loving through My Word with all you have to give.

Jesus said to him, "Have you believed because you have
seen me? Blessed are those who have not seen and yet
have believed."
John 20:29 ESV

Lord, I'll follow You Forever

Lord, I'll follow You forever,
Through the Holy Spirit,
Through Your loving faithfulness.
Following Your lead,
Planting Your gospel seeds
Praying You'll restore each soul.
Lord, I'll follow You forever,
Through the suffering streets,
Where people need to know,
Your tender love for them,
Will truly never end.
And salvation is in You alone.

Lord, I'll follow You forever,
I bear this heavy burden,
To share Your holy name.
I will study Your word,
To spread at every turn,
Let my steps walk in stride with You.
Lord I'll follow to the cross,
Where You suffered every loss,
For our own salvation to gain.
You hung in love and pain
You took away sin's stain.
To provide a way for all to come.

So the gospel shoes I'll wear,
Spreading good news everywhere,
No matter come what may,
Through persecution,
Your love will always win,
Because Jesus Christ lives within.
Lord, I'll follow you forever,
And one day You'll take me away,
From this earthly place.
Where I'll live with You forever
And look upon Your face
And newness will never be erased.

Wear shoes that are able to speed you on as you
preach the Good News of peace with God.
Ephesians 6:15 TLB

The Mountain Top

When the breeze alights joyous praise,
Through the treetops wave upon wave,

And the mountain streams gracefully run,
Their waters shimmer in the cool bright sun,

My love for you will continue and overflow,
My blessings are upon you, I bestow.

Here in my secret place my faithful ones go.
Where the leaves and streams do not question,
only faithfully follow My flow.

Here I love to come and meet with you always,
Here is where My Living water flows for all days.

What I've called you to do will clearly be made known,
For meeting in our secret place, I will walk you home.

And if the destination seems strange but crystal clear,
I have gone ahead of you there is nothing to fear.

But love me completely, I will walk with you,
Let Me shine forth and shine through.

My warrior in prayer and my servant in life,
alive in Me until the day you die...

Where you'll live with Me forever and I will always be,
Everything you've ever wanted and all
that you need, amen...God.

But when you pray, go into your room and shut the door
and pray to your Father who is in secret.
And your Father who sees in secret will reward you.
Matthew 6:6 ESV

The secret things belong unto the Lord our God:
but those things which are revealed belong unto us
and to our children forever, that we may do all the words of this law.
Deuteronomy 29:29 ESV

Eternally Lovely is Your Name

Eternally lovely is Your Name,
Only You remove the stains.
Of the sin that clouds the day,
Yes, You wipe it all away.

Through Your death on the cross,
Through suffering, and through dross.
You paid the highest cost,
So Your love will never be lost.

You rescued our very souls,
You live in us to make us whole.
And have Your guiding gracious way.
Abundantly abiding day after day.

Waiting for Your Spirit to gently resonate,
As we pray in Your beautiful Name.
Deep in quietness away from noise,
Where listening ears hear Your cherished voice.

"But the Lord is in his holy Temple;
let all the earth be silent before him."
Habakkuk 2:20

Jesus

One quiet night,
God gave us sight.

A Babe was born,
Our Savior and Lord.

Who will bring all nations to Him,
And save us all from our sin.

One quiet, holy night,
God gave us the way to eternal life...

Jesus.

Jesus

Salvation is found in no one else,
for there is no other name under Heaven
given to mankind by which we must be saved.
Acts 4:12 NIV

His Gentle Eyes

With His all-seeing eye,
God's grace will not pass you by.
He rests His healing with His gentle hand,
Within your soul, away from man.

Where He sees your every need,
And washes and cleanses by His own means.
Reminding you of His beautiful love,
And all His mercies that flow from above.

For they are new when the dawn peaks the morning,
Residing in, and descending from His own glory.
Wherein, He brings His perfect peace,
Sweet healing, and gentle release.

Reviving our souls for another day,
Walking us in His loving way.
Where our vision is given by Him,
And His lovingkindness will never end.

For I will restore your health, and your wounds
I will heal, declares the Lord.
Jeremiah 30:17 ESV

Let God

In the middle of the fight,
Is where My glory shines so bright.
If you let Me take control,
I'll walk in and restore your soul.

I will take you out of view,
Only then can I move.
Into the place where I belong,
Where your strength is completely gone.

Release everything to Me,
I know how things are meant to be.
Only then will you truly see,
My goodness flow from eternity.

My healing hand, My perfect calm,
Your Redeemer all along.
Only by My perfect will,
Will love come and the storm still.

Not by might, nor by power,
but by my Spirit says the Lord of hosts.
Zechariah 4:6 ESV

Release

Confess your sins to one another,
So, you can truly forgive your brother,
For within the hurt of the fight,
Is the burden of both sides.

May your heart receive,
The longing of your deepest need.
To love and let go,
To continue to grow.

For God longs for you to be,
Released of hurt, holy and free.
Surrounded by his gentle protection,
Receiving His plan through His eyes of perfection.

To further the kingdom only He can grow,
Only through willing vessels, in tow.
Isn't wonderful what God can do?
Through poured out servants, me, and you.

And whenever you stand praying, forgive, if you have
anything against anyone, so that your Father also who
is in heaven may forgive you your trespasses."
Mark 11:25 ESV

Love Belongs in all Places

Love belongs in all places,
Empty hearts, empty spaces.
Where evil never ever erases,
Where it will never escape seeking faces.

Because Jesus died on the cross,
We will suffer but never be lost.
For greater is His love unending,
Which will survive any doom impending.

No death, wrongdoing, can ever move,
The love God has for me and you.
So let His love flow to all places,
Fill hearts and pour into spaces.
Where it overflows downtrodden places.
And builds love for all nations.

For be assured very tribe and tongue,
Will bind together through His love.
Reaching all those who come.
The only thing that lasts is true love…
…Found only in Jesus Christ,
Who surrendered and willingly died.
Won't you come and surrender to Him.
For death in life, He opened the way to live.

Depending on Him I will always be,
He lovingly shows us people's needs.
Where I go, He leads,
My heart burns, He's all to me.
Every breath I breathe, every praise I sing.
I live in His true love, I honor My King!
Washed from my sin in the blood of the Lamb.
Always waiting, but always walking toward His promised land.

Where one day every eye will see,
Love displayed unlike any means.
Because God is the author of what was,
what is, and what is to come.
And only filled with true love.

Beloved, let us love one another, for love is from God, and
whoever loves has been born of God and knows God.
1 John 4:7 ESV

Mary Hid All These Things in Her Heart

On an ordinary day,
An angel came,
With greetings unto Mary.
She would be the mother of,
God's Son from above,
And her soul magnified the Lord.

And the angel Gabriel told Mary,
By God's Holy Spirit she would conceive.
And God's favor came to be,
And she said do as you please,
For Mary served the Lord.

Joseph received a dream,
From the angel who saw Mary,
Who told him she would birth the Song of God.
When He awoke from His sleep,
He had God's perfect peace,
And Joseph remained by her side.

And they traveled to Bethlehem to stay,
She gave birth and set Jesus in the manger to lay.
And as foretold,
By the prophet of old,
Jesus came to save the lost.

And Mary kept all these things in her heart,
And the Most High overshadowed and the
Holy Spirit did impart.
And now the people come,
From miles and some,
And receive salvation from Him.

Emanuel, God with us.
Emanuel, go and tell.
For the world He came,
And you'll never be the same,
When Jesus enters your heart!

...but Mary quietly treasured these things in her
heart and often thought about them.
Luke 2:19 TLB

To Walk with God

The wind on My treetops quietly sings through the leaves,
This is My creation resonating complete peace.

A coolness wrapped about you, a shelter in the way,
Where every heartbeat can retreat to
find rest throughout the day.

The simplicities of life are found at My hand,
Giving everything you need, at the ease of My command.

For My voice is greater than the voice of any man,
My evidence is as clear like the rain on the rivers' dance.

I am not far from those who know My name,
These are the ones who serve Me, who will never be the same.

They walk in My love and live within my Pages,
And I will walk in them throughout the end of the ages.

Where time will turn anew and things will completely change,
But if you stay in Me, all will remain the same.

Only your view will be perfect, and you will plainly see,
Everything you fought for when you walked with Me...God

I have fought the good fight, I have finished
the race, I have kept the faith.
2 Timothy 4:7 ESV

The Heart of God

The journey is long, the journey is hard,
But there is only love in the heart of God.

I have followed all my days,
I have loved in all Your ways.
Given my life to receive Yours,
Narrowed my gait to stay on Your course.

I am seeking solace in the depths of You.
I will find You sufficient all the way through.
No future, no past, nor present I see,
Can contain the love You have for me.
Nothing can separate me from Your heart,
Every piece I give You, that is broken apart.

I am standing in Your outpouring grace.
Knowing I only dimly see Your face.
The former things will wash away,
There will be no dismay.

You are the only way,
Your peace I receive until that day.
I will follow You all my days,
I will love in all Your ways.

The journey is long, the journey is hard,
But there is only love in the heart of God.

My flesh and my heart may fail, but God is the
strength of my heart and my portion forever.
Psalm 73:26

Our Coming King!

Hosanna to the King Who came,
Hosanna to the King, He will come again!
One Who rode on a donkey low,
Will return in the clouds with a mighty host!

Taking those who love Him, sincere,
Who will reign with Him, when He does appear.
Worthy is Jesus, our Lamb Who was slain,
Watch the skies, He's coming again.

We do not know the time or the day,
But with confidence we can truly say,
Jesus is the only Way,
Jesus only, has the empty grave.

Alive, risen, coming again,
For all Who are loving and living for Him.
Praise Him Who reigns on high,
Blessed are those who watch the skies...

He's coming!

Again the high priest asked him, "Are you the Christ, the Son of the
Blessed?" And Jesus said, "I am, and you will see the Son of Man seated
at the right hand of Power, and coming with the clouds of heaven."
Mark 14:61,62 ESV

Only Love

Only Love could have stayed,
Only Love truly obeyed.

Where on the cross Jesus died,
With continual love for all mankind.

Where His heart opened wide,
And He said, "Not My will, but Thine."

For a sinless Savior, God did send,
To reconcile the world to Him.

Arms opened to receive,
Forgiveness of sinners, to redeem.

For all His love He truly gave,
On that day, He is mighty to save!

I, I am the LORD, and besides me there is no savior.
Isaiah 43:11 ESV

Forevermore

In the valley of pain so deep,
That cuts like a knife, even into sleep.
Where tears overflow without end,
With a faithful hold, remains a constant Friend.

Who sees the hurt and endless grief,
Who holds you through sight unseen.
Where questions run ever deep.
And only answered with eternal peace.

May His gentleness be sown.
For He takes tender care of His own.
Delicately weaving His strength and grace,
Steadily holding you in His embrace.

Sights unseen, dreams delayed,
He will, He will, be forever stayed.
One day our ears will hear, and our eyes will see,
Such beauty where all questions will be redeemed.

Until that time, may our hope lie in,
That on the cross, we are hidden with Him.
Where all the pain of sin He bore,
That we might live forevermore.

For God has said: I will never leave you,
and I will never forsake you.
Hebrews 13:5 ESV

He Sees

I am so thankful that You see,
Each and every part of me.
Where Your Spirit searches my inner being,
Taking notice of things unseen.
Drawing me in, to Your love,
Closer and deeper, more like Your Son.

To once again, mold the clay,
In dire need of the Potter's way.
Where You again cause me to grow,
Your ways are so high, only You know.
The plan, the purpose You have for me,
So, I submit, because You see.
I lay down my life, in You I am free.

And in Your heart, I will be,
Alive and living, surrendering.

She gave this name to the Lord who spoke to her: "You are the God
who sees me," for she said, "I have now seen the One who sees me."
Genesis 16:13 NIV

His Gentle Care

Sitting in the sunlight,
Warmth, just as a fire alight.
Newness of day,
Delicate rays,
He provides the way to see.

When the sun breaks,
At the end of day,
Peace settles the night.
God sets everything aright.
He holds you and me.

Where His will,
Covers us still,
He sees the facets,
With Him life lasts.
Eternally we will be.

In a place faraway,
Yet so near, each day.
Taking gentle care,
He gets us there,
One day our eyes will see…Jesus.

He tends his flock like a shepherd:
He gathers the lambs in his arms
and carries them close to his heart;
Isaiah 40:11 NIV

Looking to You, Jesus

My heart is broken, my sin is great,
Within, it holds such heavy weight.
Where roots that do not belong,
Have taken hold and overcome.

Come in, Jesus, and chisel away,
These that reason with me, day after day.
So that my heart may be open and clean,
Filled with Your love, wholly redeemed.

Where Your holiness reflects Your living grace,
That I may walk in all Your ways.
Longing for the death of me,
Until I reach eternity.

Where all dimness will fade away,
And my heart will see You, ever stayed.
All will be clean and washed away,
May your holiness live in me until that day.

Have mercy on me, O God, according to
your unfailing love; according to your
great compassion blot out my transgressions.
Wash away all my iniquity and cleanse me
from my sin.
Psalm 51:1,2 NIV

Emmanuel

In the sky,
One star shown.
Leading to a royal throne.
Not of high or fine decree,
But kings came on bended knee.

God did send His Son to earth,
Through the virgin giving birth.
He is Christ our only peace.
Who came to live in you and me.

Peace for all who take his hand,
And follow all His commands.
Now hear this and go and tell,
God is with us Emmanuel.

Hallelujah to the King on high,
Hallelujah rest now all is nigh.
Let us come and worship him,
And rejoice in Christ our King.

...behold, wise men from the east came to Jerusalem, saying,
"Where is he who has been born king of the Jews? For we
saw his star when it rose and have come to worship him."
Matthew 2:1,2 ESV

You

Your light,
Brings hope in the night.
Emits delight,
Ceases the fight.
My heart revives.

I am still,
My heart listens at will,
You gently till,
You graciously fill.
You are Alive.

Your love remains,
Always the same.
No other Name,
No other power can claim.
Restorer of the depths of my soul.

Your Word speaks,
Delicately to me,
My eyes can't see,
But in You I am free.
In You alone I am whole.

This world fades,
And plans it has made.
My future is plain,
In You I remain.
Protector of my soul.

No other Love,
No other Friend.
You Begin where You End,
And End where You Begin.
With jealous love, You make me whole.

Arise, shine, for your light has come, and the glory of
the Lord has risen upon you. *Isaiah 60:1 ESV*

For I feel a divine jealousy for you, since I betrothed you to one husband,
to present you as a pure virgin to Christ. *2 Corinthians 11:2 ESV*

Blessed are those who keep his testimonies, who seek
him with their whole heart. *Psalm 119:2 ESV*

What Will You Bring?

What will you bring,
To a Babe born a King?
Will you bring Him purest praise,
From a heart sold out and stayed?

Or the works of your hands,
Helping nations and lands?
The meditations of your heart,
Of sole devotion, set apart?

Or the words of your mouth,
Of reflected intent, resound?
Oh, and, the depths of your soul,
Inclining to Him all that is whole?

May you lay down all that you are,
To follow all in His heart.
What will you bring,
To a Babe born a King?

For unto us a child is born,
unto us a Son is given...
Isaiah 9:6 KJV

Jesus said, "I am the way, the truth, and the life.
No one comes to the Father except through me.
John 14:6 ESV

We Three Kings

We three kings came.
Seeking His Name.
We came on bended knee,
Worshipping at His feet.

Came with much treasure,
Beyond earthly measure.
Followed the night star,
Traveling oh so far.
Went to the palace,
Blind to Herod's malice.

We found the child,
So tender and mild.
Leaving our treasure,
Gave us such pleasure.
The Angel did warn us,
Herod was dangerous.

We three kings came,
And we left changed.
The babe in the manger
Oh, what a Savior!
We'll never be the same.
We three kings came!

And going into the house, they saw the child with Mary his mother,
and they fell down and worshiped him. Then, opening their treasures,
they offered him gifts, gold and frankincense and myrrh.
Matthew 2:11 ESV

You Are Everything I Need

Your ways change my mind.
Your love is tender and kind.
You know the path I take.
Even in darkness, before I wake.

You direct me to the best way,
In You alone, I willingly stay.
When others veer the path and take another hand,
I will go with You, beside You I will stand.

For I see the difference in the ways of this world,
When people press in, whether silent or heard.
These are not your ways, and hold consequence,
I choose to stay in your protectiveness.

You know the solution, as I go along.
Your guidance will show the truth, that will correct the wrong.
When You move, I'll move, where You go, I'll go.
Your purpose and outcome will be made known.

You move me into Your light, that only You can see.
For You see the unseen, and desire others to see Christ in me.
So, move me on Your path and use me as you will.
For Your gentleness and omnipotence, you will fulfill.

Where all will be resolved, and at the end of days,
All will be known, everything displayed.
Until that time, I'll walk with You, waiting as You lead.
All will be corrected because You have everything I need.

Your word is a lamp to my feet and a light to my path.
Psalm 119:105 ESV

59

You Thought of Me

In a dream,
Or would it seem?
God had a plan,
For you to hold my hand.
A tender thought,
Lovingly brought.

A dream He did hide,
Until His perfect time.
When love was sweet,
In deepest need.
Just when the thought,
Was almost lost.

God brought pleasure,
Beyond earthly measure.
To have to hold,
God made Himself known.
I will not be alone,
He brought my heart a home.

Time was seemingly,
Long without meaning.
I held on to You,
And Your timely truth.
You saw my deepest need,
You have taken care of me.

My heart melds to
my love alone,
Where I am free to shed my soul.
For You have given to
me beyond measure,
A gift I will completely treasure.

It was You all along,
It was You Who was strong.
When I was weak,
And on my knees.
You answered my prayer,
You were always there.

Now I will have and hold,
My love, and grow old.
And remember Your ways,
And Your promises that remain.
I will never be the same,
I have given You my name.

The king's heart is a stream of water in the hand
of the Lord; he turns it wherever he will.
Proverbs 21:1 ESV

Behold, I have engraved you on the palms of my hands;
your walls are continually before me.
Isaiah 49:16 ESV

In the Middle of the Night

In the middle of the night,
I know You hold me tight,
And I can't get away from Your love.

So I will lay in Your arms,
Safe from all harm,
And remember the Words of Your Son.

Rest, now, My child for I love you so,
I will never leave you, nor let you go.
Be still and rest your head, as you lay on your bed,
I will keep you in perfect peace.

I love the gentle noise,
Of Your tender voice,
Always speaking to me.
I will open my hand, to receive,
The tenderness of Your peace.

Blessed are You, Oh, Lord my Savior and King!
With my tender voice I do gently sing.
Praises to Your Name, for You never change,
I love Your sacrifice to me.

Be still, be still, and rest my soul,
My heart is set on Thee, my Lord.
I will lie here and sleep,
In perfect peace,
As you watchfully gaze over me.

You keep him in perfect peace
whose mind is stayed on you,
because he trusts in you.
Isaiah 26:3 ESV

God's Butterfly

A butterfly dances around,
Leaving beauty where it is found.
Bringing youthful and elderly smiles,
With memories that continue for miles.
Leaving behind a glimpse of God's glory,
Such a small but profound part of His creation story.

Its shining ray of hope,
Seems to flow from God's kaleidoscope.
Radiant and winsome ever sweet,
Full and colorful always unique.

As it turns and flies away,
It leaves a part of it to stay.
A new life is born again,
Assurance of witness without end.
For God begins and ends each day,
And He knows the seasons without delay.

His time and beauty are ever new,
Ten thousand years are only a few.
For soon all brilliance of color will remain,
All because we are born again.
Changed and forever, not the same,
And we will live where glory is gain.

But do not overlook this one fact, beloved, that with the Lord
one day is as a thousand years, and a thousand years as one day.
2 Peter 3:8 ESV

Jesus, Heir of all Things

Of beauty, grace, and glory,
He is our love story.

Living to receive,
All who cleave,
In purity and strength,
In courage, unashamed.

Walking in meekness,
Strength in weakness,
All for above reproach,
Clean, white garments alone, approach.

The radiance of Him.
The Heir of all things.

But in these last days he has spoken to us by his
Son, whom he appointed the heir of all things,
through whom also he created the world.
Hebrews 1:2 ESV

Jesus Builds the House

As the wave needs the shore,
So, my love to you forevermore.
And so the tender dance begins,
And goes from new to gentle friend.

Wherein I find someone unique.
Seemingly, built just for me.
As we explore His plan alone.
Take my hand and we'll journey home.

To be at my side as we walk together.
Where two are better in His plan forever.
To build and help and learn and grow.
God and His ways perfect how we go.

Where trust and lean, beautifully team,
And His ways strengthen you and me.
As together we better portray.
An impact made to last and stay.

As furtherance of His holy ways.
Wherein He guides to shower the days.
With words and works that will only last,
As we take the less traveled, narrow path.

Leaving behind His beacon of love,
Others will know the way because,
The testimony we have is true,
For Jesus builds the house within me and you.

Two are better than one,
because they have a good return for their labor:
Ecclesiastes 4:9 NIV

Follow

Is it so hard to follow me?
When I died so that you could live free?
Free of conscience cut too deep.
Free to be all you are supposed to be?

As the breeze blows through the trees,
Listen as my voice encompasses thee.
I am a breath away,
I love you day after day.

Oh, in the beauty of stillness lain,
My foundation of knowledge I give and maintain.
No better life, be rooted in Me,
The world will never outshine My glory.

My Word will never return void,
I love you My child no longer toil.
Your freedom lies in every breath.
So grasp to Me I know what's best.

I will never be ashamed of you,
I will show myself in all you go through.
Only look into My eyes,
Where My peace and joy give no compromise.

For all the world will fade and fall.
But failure will not come to those who call,
On my Name in perfect plea,
I gave my life so you could follow Me.

As Jesus passed on from there, he saw a man called
Matthew sitting at the tax booth, and he said to him,
"Follow me." And he rose and followed him.
Matthew 9:9 ESV

You See Us Through

You are big, I am small,
You are the Creator over all.
You are the Foundation alone,
Alive, living, precious Stone.

When all else falls and fails,
You will remain, You prevail.
A secure, safe, dwelling place,
For all who abide in Your saving grace.

Where feet may slip and give way,
But always righted by You, Who stay,
Beside Your children day after day,
Leading and guiding and receiving always.

So we look to You our only Foundation.
You alone hold our salvation.
The Cornerstone and Builder of life,
Found in the heart of each child...

Who surrenders their will to You,
Who perfects the plan, to see us through.

And I am sure of this, that he who began a good work in you
will bring it to completion at the day of Jesus Christ.
Philippians 1:6 ESV

His Light Sown

What lies ahead of me?
Light for my eyes to see.
Sown solely unto me,
By my Savior, who gently leads.

Where no other foot will go,
A plan only He does know.
With my steps, I will go,
And walk where His light is sown.

For there is only one of me,
In comfort knowing, He truly sees,
Everything I'll ever need.
He lights the path ahead of me.

And the joy He gives is tenderly sown,
As the heart alights to those who follow...Jesus

Light is sown for the righteous;
and joy for the upright in heart!
Psalm 27:11 ESV

What's To Do?

Do what lies before,
No need to question, is there more?
For it takes away the precious worth,
Of what, for this time, I have birthed.

For you of are great value to Me.
And what you are doing is what I see.
So, walk and know that your faith,
Is the gift I've given, while you wait...

For those things that lie ahead,
And they will come, when you've been fed,
By my great and loving hand,
So you will be ready to stand...

On the rise of the next season,
Where I lovingly give, within reason,
Everything you'll ever need,
So do what lies in front of thee.

Therefore, as you received Christ Jesus the Lord, so walk in him.
Colossians 2:6 ESV

Accepted

Never ashamed, nor unclaimed,
For I have given you My Name.
With Me you can rest and talk,
Hold My hand, take long walks.

Come unto Me in confident hope,
For I will never let you go.
All your thoughts will deepen our love,
Your prayers will ascend as a dove.

For I will always hold you dear,
No need to ever fear.
My heart holds you forevermore,
And mirrors an open door.

Always welcome every day,
Only lovingly abide, come what may.
You are accepted just as you are,
For you are the beloved of My heart.

He made us accepted in the Beloved.
Ephesians 1:6 NKJV

For You

Come now everything exists,
By reason of God's omnipotence.
Nothing arises from mere chance,
God controls all circumstance.

Is it darkness or is it light?
Is it wrong or is it right?
Is it moral or is it not?
Is it God's, or man's mortal thought?

A compass never tells a lie.
Character, it rectifies.
Its direction safely leads,
Where every soul has a need.

To be lost no more,
To be rescued from war.
To know the Creator in the deepest parts.
Where His peace can reign in every heart.

He lays the path for you to take His hand,
He alone knows the perfect plan!
Even before time began,
God thought of every man.

Lift your eyes to the cross,
Where Jesus suffered every loss.
Will you take hold of His cost?
He doesn't want you lost.

He came to the earth so all could receive Him.
There is nothing more to reason.
You would not exist if it wasn't for Him.
He alone can save you from sin!

Won't you come now?

And saying, "The time is fulfilled, and the kingdom of God is at hand;
repent and believe in the gospel."
Mark 1:15 ESV

Sow in Jesus

With bitter jealousy and selfish ambition aside,
Come to the harvest where righteousness thrives.

Sown in peace by those who are pure,
Those who are gentle, full of mercy unfurled.

Open to reason through humility and love,
Woven by those, who seek God's wisdom above.

Bearing good fruit from a life so sincere,
From an impartial heart who knows God's way so clear.

A harvest of righteousness, never uprooted,
But loving and peaceful by God who approves.

And a harvest of righteousness is sown in
peace by those who make peace.
James 3:18 ESV

Continue On

What to do, beside of you?
When one does not live the Truth.
You may not even be aware,
But they can be, right there.

So let your wheat bare golden grain,
Soaking in His glorious rain.
To give and share, bringing many in,
For this is refreshing, over and again.

In the end, He will display,
He, who walks, in His ways,
For whoever loves the Son, and shines so bright,
He will gather into His barn full of light.

Continue in Jesus' arms,
Knowing He will keep you strong.
Helping you along the way,
Be His wheat, come what may.

Let both grow together until the harvest,
and at harvest time I will tell the reapers,
Gather the weeds first and bind them in bundles to be burned,
but gather the wheat into my barn.
Matthew 13: 30 ESV

The Dagger

The dagger that is after me,
Cuts my heart and cuts it deep.
It was never meant for me,
For it only makes me bleed.

But Your blood runs through my veins,
Where no poison can remain.
You have given me Your mind,
And have readied me from behind.

So, I refuse the daggers that want to settle in,
That tear and divide away within.
I'll open my hand and let them go
Jesus defends, this I know.

When I hurt and am vulnerable,
Of being stripped of all I know.
Underneath lies Jesus' hand,
In His victory I can stand.

I know I plainly see,
War and battle surround me.
And the daggers may continue through time,
But my Savior has said, "You are mine."

For you shall not go out in haste, and you shall not go in flight,
for the LORD will go before you, and the God
of Israel will be your rear guard.
Isaiah 52:12 ESV

Loving Lord

I walk in You, Jesus, the resurrection,
For You are alive, may I be Your reflection.

Please help me not go astray,
For I know You are the One True Way.

Your faithfulness You do send,
Even in the lion's den.

When tests and trials do assail,
You will help me, You never fail.

You made me Your temple when I asked You in,
Pattern me to You, over and again.

Until the time I can look upon Your face,
Continue to surround me with unending grace.

I love You, my Lord, You're so good to me,
For You have given me everything I need.

No longer do I call you servants, for the servant does not know
what his master is doing; but I have called you friends, for all that
I have heard from my Father I have made known to you.
John 15:15 ESV

Stand

Just as the rising of the sun,
Persecution will surely come.
But God has raised you up,
And called you to drink this cup.

Look back to where you began,
When you took Jesus' hand.
Ponder what He's pulled you through,
And pray that others will come too.

For friends and loved ones are watching you.
Will you continue to journey though?
Jesus' presence is your strength, your fortress,
His Word within you wields confidence.

When in sorrow, joy, or pain,
Let Jesus in You forever reign.
Others will see your steadfast walk,
And receive the words you truthfully talk.

For your deeds will be fully known,
When you enter Jesus' home.
So, when persecution comes to you,
This momentous affliction has purpose, too.

Imitate Christ and do his will,
His purpose you will fulfill.
Others will follow of whom you didn't even know,
When the love of Christ enraptures your soul.

Indeed, all who desire to live a godly life in
Christ Jesus will be persecuted
2 Timothy 3:12

Arise

On the last day, we will rise,
If we have died in Christ.
And this truth was displayed,
When Jesus raised Lazarus from the grave.

Jesus loved his friend dearly,
He wept aloud with Martha and Mary.
But long before He was crucified,
He prayed to His Father, calling Lazarus to arise.

Here he showed everyone,
He is the Resurrection, God's only Son.
He is the Life given for all men,
No one else under Heaven, yes and amen!

And not so long after this,
Our Father exchanged Jesus for the wages of sin.
Here He suffered sin's greatest debt,
And those who loved him, wept and wept.

After separation from His Father in Heaven,
He took His Life back; He is the Resurrection.
He is all-powerful, omnipotent, glorious,
He came to life again, risen and victorious.

Allowing those born twice in Christ to arise,
For death has no power over the Resurrection and the Life!

Martha said to him, "I know that he will rise again in the resurrection
on the last day. Jesus said to her, "I am the resurrection and the life.
Whoever believes in me, though he die, yet shall he live,
and everyone who lives and believes in me shall never die.
Do you believe this?
John 11:24-26 ESV

Your Hand

Here I am,
I take Your hand.
Your servant You see,
You're so beautiful to me.

I lift my praise,
My hands I raise.
You are good,
With all things understood.

I place myself at Your feet,
I know in You I am complete.
All my days,
All Your ways.
No other path,
I'm safe from attack.

Through the day and night seasons,
On Your road I need no reason.
Only to trust to love to bask,
Your eternal care continually lasts.
Your attention is perfect toward me.
In Your perfect will, I'll forever be.

For I am sure that neither death nor life, no angels nor rulers,
nor things present nor things to come, nor powers, nor height
nor depth, nor anything else in all creation, will be able to
separate us from the love of God in Christ Jesus our lord.
Romans 8:38,39 ESV

Greater Than Gold

Forgiveness carries the highest price,
Given by God's only Son, a powerful sacrifice.
An offering poured out because of love,
Wrong made right through Jesus' blood.

It cannot be bought or sold,
But it's worth is far greater than gold.
For it brings freedom only seen,
When freely given and without price received.

Extended beyond human comprehension,
By open arms of surrendered extension.
To the one who doesn't deserve grace,
And also, the other who reflects his face.

But oh, the release it with certainty sows,
When one fully knows.
The penalty lifted, utterly gone,
And the joy Jesus gives at that moment and on.

Only then can the heart truly contain,
Such a fullness none can explain.
The most refined, priceless treasure of all,
The voice of my Savior, when I answer His call...
To forgive others and to receive His forgiveness.

"For this is my blood of the covenant,
which is poured out for many for the forgiveness of sins."
Matthew 26:28 ESV

Blameless...

means no shamefulness.
Innocence stayed,
Holiness inlaid.
A thorough cleanse,
From deep within.
A washing clean,
With precious blood unseen.
A coal of fire,
To burn the mire.
To give the mind,
From the beginning of time.
Of the One Who loves us,
Of the One Who rescues us.
Into life with Him,
Surrounded by sin.
But free from chains,
And unwelcome stains.
To tell others He reigns,
And He's coming again!
In the midst of chaos,
He restores us.

Only let go and grab hold.
Of the One who pulls,
Up out of the clay.
Into a home forever stayed.
Oh, He loves us, He loves us still.
He gave us His all, He
gave us His will.
To die in our place,
He loves to embrace,
His children so dear,
So draw near.
Hear His voice,
Make the choice.
To love Him still,
To do God's will.
A life surrendered in Him,
Sanctifies within.
It's a journey of love, only begin.

Even as he chose us in him before the foundation of the world,
that we should be holy and blameless before him. In love he
predestined us for adoption to himself as sons through Jesus
Christ, according to the purpose of his will, to the praise of his
glorious grace, with which he has blessed us in the Beloved.
Ephesians 1:4-6 ESV

God Continues Our Journey

I'm at a halt.
But You are not.
You're always moving to make a way,
So, I'll continue to walk in You all day.

Words, no words,
But Your Word is strong,
Living and powerful to carry on.
Thorough in correction, dividing right from wrong.

Stuck, but secure,
Unsure of surroundings.
But You know the heart's deepest reserves.
You guide the path, You know the twists and turns.

Free, anywhere in grace,
Where sin is forgiven and erased.
Your will be done, I follow You,
Questions answered when I see anew.

For this light momentary affliction is preparing for us an eternal
weight of glory beyond all comparison, as we look not to the things
that are seen but to the things that are unseen. For the things that
are seen are transient, but the things that are unseen are eternal.
2 Corinthians 4:17,18 ESV

God Showers His Bride

The bride walks to the Groom,
She wonders, is there any room?
In His heart for a lowly one,
For in her heart, she loves the Son.

As she walks, she meets His eyes,
All doubt fades as she does realize.
He is everything she will ever need,
She is now free to release,   .

Her every longing and every desire,
Into His hands, that never tire.
Where she will be safe and find,
His love will last for a lifetime.

Hallelujah! For the LORD our God the Almighty reigns! Let us
rejoice and exalt and give him the glory, for the marriage of the
Lamb has come, and his Bride has made herself ready; it was
granted her to clothe herself with fine linen, bright and pure –
Revelation 19:6-8 ESV

The Shepherd's Evening

On a lowly hillside,
God's grace did abide,
And the shepherds watched their sheep.

The sky was so calm,
No sound, no alarm,
And the night was filled with peace.

When suddenly God's glory,
Flooded the field.
And His angel from Heaven beautifully appeared.
And the Shepherds felt afraid until the angel did say,
"Fear not, I bring you Good News!"
Luke 2:10 ESV

All people, all nations will rejoice,
For a Savior has been born Who is Christ the Lord!
And this is the sign:
The one for all time,
The Babe in the manger does lay!

And joy filled the shepherds' hearts
At the message the angel did impart,
As the sky resounded with praise.

For suddenly on the lowly hillside,
Appeared God's heavenly choir.
And the shepherds heard what they said!

"Glory to God in the highest!
And peace on earth to all who please him!"
Luke 2:14 ESV

Heaven's angels went away,
And the shepherds did say,
Let us go to Bethlehem.

They found the sign the angel gave.
The babe lying in the hay,
And they made the message known to all.

Today your heart can be filled with joy!
For salvation comes through this baby boy!
For the angel proclaimed the sign,
Through Jesus, salvation is yours and mine!

And in the same region there were shepherds out in the field,
keeping watch over their flock by night. And an angel of the
Lord appeared ...and said to them, "For unto you is born this
day in the city of David a Savior, who is Christ the Lord."
Luke 2:8-11 ESV

Alive in Him

Christ suffered in the flesh,
So we can receive His very best.
A new life, gained through Him,
Beautiful identity, ceased from sin.

To be alive in Him, to His will,
Where His purpose for you He will fulfill.
For the darkness of sin is left in the past,
This brand new life will last and last.

And the Judge will judge the earth,
So please be found in His new birth.
For His Gospel makes the dead alive,
And His Holy Spirit helps you abide.

The end is near, stay sober and pray.
Love one another deeply, day after day.
Be hospitable, serve the Lord with a smile,
For your speech and service will travel eternity's miles.

And rejoice at the trials to come,
For your identity is in Christ, who paid Your ransom.
And judgement will begin at the house of God,
The disobedient will suffer, speak the Gospel on and on.

And trust to Him your very soul.
You are more valuable than you know!
For He Who created you refines you with fire,
He walks alongside you, He never tires!

And, "If the righteous is scarcely saved, what will become of the
ungodly and the sinner?" Therefore let those who suffer according to
God's will entrust their souls to a faithful Creator while doing good.
1 Peter 4:18,19 ESV

Alpha and Omega

Alpha and Omega, Beginning and End,
Jesus, our Savior, free of sin.
Freely came for us to freely receive,
Eternal life, with eyes to see the unseen.

A circumcision of the heart,
To refine a purity set apart,
To serve the One Who began all things.
And will see to the closing of all ends.

He is the Start, He is the Finish,
He came to live within us.
He died and rose again,
Yes, He is the Beginning and the End.

Where will your end be?
Can you reason with eternity?
Bow down and surrender your life,
You will live and never die!

For you will see Him as He is,
Come to the Start so you can Finish!

"I am the Alpha and the Omega, the first and
the last, the beginning and the end."
Revelation 22:13 ESV

Jesus Cares

Jesus cares, yes, He does,
For He died for all of us.
He bore our sin and pain,
So we could be born again.

Every care, every need,
You can lay at His feet.
He carried all our anxieties,
He came to live in you and me.

He causes the wind to blow,
He knows where His Holy Spirit goes.
He loves when we invite Him in,
Even angels rejoice over this!

His blood blots out our sin,
Won't you simply come to Him?
Where your life will be forever new,
All because He died for you.

When someone becomes a Christian,
He becomes a brand new person inside.
He is not the same anymore. A new life has begun!
2 Corinthians 5:17 TLB

Our God Who loves Us

Oh, the depths of God's heart,
His love will never depart.
His holiness does cleanse within,
As He washes away tendency toward sin.

Making our hearts a holy place,
Where we can safely partake,
The words of His mouth that He gives,
To all who surrender to His holiness.

For within the pages of His love,
He sends beauty from above.
No longer ashes or an old pot of clay,
But a vessel of use by Him day after day.

Set apart, to stay by His side,
To quietly remain at His feet and abide.
For because of His perfect poured out life,
You can partake food given by Him until the end of time.

Where He fills you up with oil and wine,
Into new wineskins eternal, divine.
For there is no other table in which to dine,
Only the one where He says, "You are Mine."

Simon Peter replied, "Master, to whom shall we go?
You alone have the words that give eternal life."
John 6:68 ESV

Listen

Sit closely, quietly, in the morning light,
Listen for My voice, I AM right here by your side.
Waiting for your thoughts to solely turn to Me,
And your heart yielded and open, where I alone see.

Here in our secret place, I will meet with you,
Only wait for My voice, I speak only truth.
Peace, I will give you for the steps you take each day,
My courage awaits you, only ask and pray.

You are never alone, never lonely you will be,
Because I will walk beside you, giving joy continually.
Even in the circumstances, you can't figure out,
Know that I AM with you, forever without a doubt.

You are My child, in Me you are free,
For I will always love you, unconditionally.
So listen for My voice, I will never let you go,
Nor will I leave you, and My Word says, so.

The LORD appeared to him from far away. I have loved you with an
everlasting love; therefore I have continued my faithfulness to you.
Jeremiah 31:3 ESV

His Grace is Enough

Everything in my heart,
You know every part.
The fears and the hesitancies among,
The shy and embarrassed ones.

But You see a different side,
One that desperately longs to try.
To obey and do Your holy will,
And glory in all You fulfill.

So I will kneel and abide,
In You, I will gently hide.
Laying before You all of my heart,
I know You will fill every part.

And when I walk and when I stand,
I know it will be by Your hand.
My years will reveal Your beautiful plan,
Because I placed my heart in Your hands.

He will cover you with his pinions, and under
his wings you will find refuge;
his faithfulness is a shield and buckler.
Psalm 91:4 ESV

Your Eyes

I stepped into Your shadow,
You became my light.
My vision blurred,
You gave me Your sight.
To bless me with things unseen,
That only occur within Your means.

I looked up to what was not,
Then you revealed, after I sought.
For Your work is complete,
Deepen Your love inside of me.
Where only Your priceless treasures lay,
That will take me to see You one day.

Where the works of my hands and meditations of my heart,
Will go before me and we will never part.

Give her the fruit of her hands,
and let her works praise her in the gates.
Proverbs 31:31ESV

Last, But Chosen

I will remain at Your side,
To trust and lovingly abide.
For no good can ever come,
When you forget where you came from.

From the One who made you with intimate deign,
And dressed you in righteousness from the beginning of time.
Who loves you more than life itself,
And who died to give you His wealth.

A heavenly home filled with precious treasure,
And beauty too immense to humanly measure.
Who will aright all things to His will,
And bring His purposes to fulfill.

Where no one will ever hunger or thirst,
And all will be satisfied who are not first.
For our crowns will bless His name,
And in His righteousness, we will be changed.

To forever live anew,
Where all will be well because He loves you.
He will remain at your side,
Only trust and lovingly abide.

So the last will be first, and the first last.
Matthew 20:16 ESV

Who Sees Inside of You?

Who can see inside of you?
All our veins and vessels
running through?
Who knows the hairs
on your head?
And your thoughts as
you lay on your bed?

For life is more than
food and drink,
Running inside you and me.
This is what Jesus came to show,
His Word is what causes growth.

Look to the beauty, enjoyed
through the ages,
The creatures and
scenes He displays.
For a day is like a
thousand years,
Only the Father knows
when Jesus will appear.

The trumpet sound
will break the air,
Are you ready, have
you laid bare?
Everything that you are,
Into our Savior's loving heart?

Making yourself ready
for His return
With your flame afire,
with desire that burns.
In the end, this will
all pass away,
The one who sees you
will come to stay.

Turn now to Him, He
loves you so,
It is true, all of creation groans.
Oh, if you could trust
Him trust Him so,
For all things He does know.

Never will He tire of
taking care of you.
But He can't do it if you
don't know the truth.
Jesus died for you and
he is coming again,
Only to rescue those
living for Him.

He sees inside of you
What now will you do?
Open His Word and
read His truth,
Where the blood in His
veins spilled out for you.

But he said to them, "I have food to eat
that you do not know about."
John 4:32 ESV

And no creature is hidden from his sight, but all are naked and
exposed to the eyes of him to whom we must give account.
Hebrews 4:13 ESV

You Must Stand

Where are the faithful
in the land?
Who genuinely take
our Father's hand?
Are they continual
in staying true?
Do they love righteousness
and see it through?

When times are clouded
by religion,
Falsities and men, causing
derision, division.
What is false seems true,
What does the Bible say to do?

Test everything with God's word.
It divides, a strong sword.
Testing the hearts of men.
Correction, causing
them to strengthen.

If we leave, if we give up,
What will become of
the faithful ones?
Scattered abroad,
no longer whole,
Everything gone,
burdened in soul.

People will laugh
without escape
And the world will say,
it was all fake.

But we are His people, His
sheep in His pasture,
We know there is an
eternity after.
Even if it hurts, even
if things break.
We will stand strong,
whatever it takes.

He will not forsake us, oh,
He loves us so much!
Will we remember the things
He has done for us?
Remember and recall
all His faithful deeds,
His testing shows His genuine
love for you and me.
One day all will be seen,
one day all will be known.
Did you sow to produce
goodness in the light of
your Heavenly Home?

So even if you're tired,
even so faint.
Don't give up, Jesus
sees you dear saint.
He will rescue, He will behold.
Every faithful sheep in
His precious fold.

I am coming soon. Hold fast what you have, so that no one
may seize your crown. The one who conquers, I will make him a
pillar in the temple of my God. Never shall he go out of it, and
I will write on him the name of my God, and the name of the
city of my God, the new Jerusalem, which comes down from
my God out of heaven, and my own new name. He who has
an ear, let him hear what the Spirit says to the churches.'
Revelation 3:11-13 ESV

Doer

Do what lies before,
No need to question, is there more?
For it takes away the precious worth,
Of what for this time, I have birthed.

For you are of great value to me,
And what you are doing is what I see.
So walk and know that your faith,
Is the gift I've given while you wait...

For those things that lie ahead,
And they will come when you've been fed.
By My great and loving hand.
So you will be ready to stand...

On the rise of the next season,
Where I lovingly give within reason.
Everything you'll ever need,
So do what lies in front of thee.

Be doers of the word, and not hearers only,
deceiving yourselves.
James 1:22 ESV

Where Are You Planted?

Are you planted firmly in the Lord?
Abiding through any and all accord?
Branching out, holding firm,
So others can watch and learn?

Producing shoots brilliant in color,
So they will know there is no other.
And fruit that bears so bountifully,
Where they can taste and truly see,

God is the producer of all good things,
His power resounds majestically.
Causing wind to sway through leaves,
Where roots are strong, able to cleave.

For there is only One True Vine,
Who grafted us into eternity's time,
So we could abide and be able to produce,
Good works to bring others God's Good News, Jesus!

Let your roots grow down into him and draw up nourishment
from him. See that you go on growing in the Lord, and become
strong and vigorous in the truth you were taught. Let your lives
overflow with joy and thanksgiving for all he has done.
Colossians 2:7 ESV

Restful Pasture

There is a gate to enter in,
Through a gentle Savior and Friend.
Who provides perfect pasture,
Morning, evening, noon, and thereafter.

Here the Savior knows each name,
And each one is truly grateful they came.
They listen to His voice assured,
For they have protection in His pasture.

The Shepherd feeds them with His Word.
And He gives them rest assured.
Here they learn and grow,
The value of sitting at His feet, they know.

So, in and out they come and go.
To share His love and saving Gospel.
To bring others into His sheepfold,
So all will know the salvation He holds.

Given freely to all who come.
Who enter by the only door, God's only Son.
Who came to rescue all men,
And give them new pastures over and again.

I am the door. If anyone enters by me, he will
be saved and will go in and out
and find pasture.
John 10:9

Prayerful Notes:

Printed in the United States
by Baker & Taylor Publisher Services